Ask yourself...

Is everything done by design?
Do we meet people on purpose or by convenient chance?
Is it in His long-term plan to cross the paths of those we need when we need them or they need us?
People enter your life for a Season or a Lifetime.
The trick is determining which one it is...

Dedication:

Folded fingers, late night conversations, early morning texts. Laughs, smiles, kisses, and hugs. Support with advice, affection, jokes, and tears. Thankful for it all at the end of the day, because I learned something that I needed to learn about me. That I want love and I deserve to be loved. When the bricks you place to build your dream doesn't finish construction, do you tear it down and do you start over or do you continue to try and build fighting for your dream?

Life's journey is filled with trials and tribulations. With those trails comes the people meant to affect you. We all cross paths for a season or a lifetime to make a difference in the lives of others. To teach a lesson or to learn one. You were the best friend I never saw coming and the one who was the muse for this story. May you find what your heart desires and the peace needed so you can enjoy it. I wish we could've been a lifetime but I will always remember our Season.

Forever in my prayers as you hold a place in my heart, you were my first Boaz. And I was your transitional woman.

The Intro

The transitional woman lives within us all, she can be anyone. She can be your teacher, your sister, the lady at the grocery store, or the woman sitting next to you in church. The thing is we don't all tap into her nor have a WANT to be her. All women are not willing to put themselves in that position to help others heal, grow, or develop. Most times the transitional woman appears when you least expect it. Her purpose is to help; her purpose is to show; her purpose is to support, until the one in transition no longer needs her. Then upon his next try at a relationship it flourishes and the transitional woman knows that it is because of who she was for him and how she fulfilled her role in his life. It could be two months or two years. Her insatiable habit of trying to fix or repair them draws her to them like worker bees to the queen. It's not physical and it's not emotional...it's something else.

Ironic how I find myself in this role and my Mother in her wisdom gave me my name. I laugh at it a lot because I wonder if she had any inclination that I would be this person.

Helping others heal when I can't heal myself. Fixing the broken, while I'm held together by scotch tape and loose string. But then again, it's not really about me is it. It's about fulfilling my calling and being that rock for those whose path I cross or cross mine. Transition and change are unrelenting and traveling that road alone is tough. Man was not meant to be alone, that's why God gave Adam ... Eve. But there is no passage that speaks of a woman finding a man. I am your comfort, your shoulder, your voice of reason when you find yourself in that dark corner of your mind... contemplating.

The one in transition? She learns to love everything about him...even the things she hates. She accepts him for who he is, what he is, and where he is in life. She puts her efforts of encouragement into him, only wanting him to be the best he can be. She wants him to reach every goal he has ever set for himself and exceed even his own expectations. Through the ups and downs, she rocks with him (as long as he is doing things in a positive nature). In the end, he walks away and takes all that she has done for him. Not only does he take it with him, he takes it to make him a better man for the next woman he is with. And it never fails that the next woman he becomes involved with he marries while the transitional woman is left standing in the shadow. Sometimes she's hurt and sometimes she's proud that she was able to push him to be a good man, a better man, even if it wasn't in the cards for that man to be with her.

How do you become a transitional woman? Well beautiful, it's not something you become, it's just something you are born to be. Selfless love and the want to see others happy, as the Powers that Be meant for it to be. It's not a cut and dry situation unfortunately but it's always understood that no new friendship is developed without the knowledge that it won't last. The realization that once your purpose is served he or she will move on without you. And before you know it, that healed heart will open for the next person and a new chapter will begin.

Now, I won't lie to you about one thing. Sometimes it hurts as you watch that chapter of your life come to an end. But sometimes watching that broken or bruised spirit mend and progress fills your heart as if things had worked out for you. All in all, you should prepare yourself accordingly. Is that something to be proud of? I can't be sure to be honest. I just think it's just what it is. I understand my role as the transitional woman and time and time again the one who needs me appears in my life. And this time was no different than the last.

So, let me formally introduce myself. Hello. My name is Peace Willows and I am known as the transitional woman.

The Wake-Up

His name was Shamar and after 20 years of loving the same woman in a marriage he thought was solid, she walked out on him. He had no clue that she had become someone else because he always saw what he wanted to see when it came to her. That beautiful 20-year-old woman he met in college. When he looked at her, he didn't see the twinge of gray at the nape of her neck or the small wrinkles at the corners of her mouth. He didn't see the sadness in her eyes or hear the missing ring of joy in her laugh. He thought everything was just as good if not better than the day her married her. But she was not the same. She had grown to believe that she had missed the things in life she now saw their young adult children experiencing because she married a man that she no longer loved.

The signs were there. The signs had been there for the past eight months but Shamar didn't notice until he came home after work thinking his dinner would be on the table waiting for him. What Shamar found was nothing but silence. No sounds of water running in the kitchen sink, no singing from the tv room, and no smells of tonight's dinner. Silence. Only silence. No one ever knows the true quiet of silence until you're standing in it. No one notices how final the absence of sound is until it is swallowing you whole from the outside in. Filling your lungs with the air of the last breaths the one you loved left behind.

He walked around the 3500-square foot home that he shared with Jessica just this morning with the thought that maybe she had been out running errands and would be back soon with some takeout. He checked the rooms downstairs then made his way to the master suite. When he opened the door, nothing was out of place. He walked over to her closet as the door was ajar. As he stepped in, he saw it then. The drawers which held her intimates were pulled open. Her hangers were empty of her clothes. Some were even on the floor like she had packed her things in a hurry so that she wouldn't run into him. And just like the empty hangers, her shoe cubby followed suite. Her shelves were bare and her jewelry was gone. Everything was gone. Jessica was gone. Shamar fell against the wall and stared at the walk-in closet in disbelief. Not knowing what to feel or what to do he just sat...in silence.

The Meeting

Walking out of the bookstore I bump into a man and drop everything I have in my hands. He instantly drops to one knee to pick them up as soon as I do.

"My apologies, I was not paying attention to where I was going." I say.

"No problem, neither was I honestly. " he admits.

We both pick up a little of everything and as we stand he offers me the books from his hands.

"Thank you, you didn't have to do that."

"Nonsense. What kind of man would I be to not assist a beautiful woman? My mama raised me better than that." He offers his hand and says, "Hello. My name is Shamar Michaels."

"Hello. I'm Peace."

"Just, Peace? No last name?"

"Peace Willows." I say with a smile.

"Well Ms. Willows, that's a very unique name. I'm sure there's some sort of history behind it."

"There is."

"But I guess you're not going to expand on it." Shamar says with a smirk on his face as his eyes scan my frame.

"You guessed correctly." I reply as I watch his eyes work their way back up to my face. "Are you finished?"

"Excuse me?" he smiles acting as if he has no idea what I'm referring to.

"Are you finished? Measuring me up."

"Oh, you saw that? As a matter of fact, I am."

"And?"

"And what?" he smiles wider as he realizes this has turned into a little game.

"And, do you like what you see?"

"I must admit that it is definitely a "Peace" of amazing work. Pun intended."

"Imagine that. Well Shamar, thank you again for your assistance. Enjoy the rest of your day."

"Ummm, excuse me Peace. I may be overreaching at this point but I'd be kicking myself in the ass later if I didn't at least attempt this. Would you like to go to dinner?"

"Dinner? You haven't even asked for my number or even if I was involved with someone already."

"While I previewed God's amazing work, I peeked at your left hand and noticed it to be vacant of a ring. Then I said to myself, 'Self, if a woman this fine does not have a ring on her finger you might have a chance.' So, I decided to try my luck. Was I incorrect to be so presumptuous that you would be available to have dinner with me, tonight?"

"Oh, so now it's dinner, tonight?"

"If you are available."

"I didn't have any plans. I guess I can be persuaded to join you for dinner."

"What type of food do you like?"

"I'm partial to Greek."

"Great, there's a nice cozy place off of East Coastal by the name of Theodosia's. Let's meet there at 7:30pm."

I check my watch to see that it's 3:15pm. "Sounds good. See you at 7:30pm Shamar."

"Most definitely Peace. Most definitely."

I turn to walk away towards my car and make sure not to look back in his direction. I get to my car and place my items in the backseat then climb in. after I start my car, I pull slowly from the parking space and look left towards the bookstore. To my surprise, Shamar is still standing there looking in my direction. He raises his arm to wave and as I pull off, he walks into the bookstore. I turn my music up and drive home basically on autopilot because I'm thinking about what I'm going to wear tonight for this impromptu dinner date.

Now we all know what's in the back of my mind, right? What question is running around on repeat over and over again. Is this another case of me being the transitional woman? Right now, I can't be sure right now but it will be revealed soon. It always is. I reach my destination and exit my car, grabbing the books and bags in the backseat.

"Alright Peace, let's see what's in this closet."

The Date

I drive over to the restaurant to meet Shamar and see that it's actually only twenty minutes from my townhouse. Its located next to a small shopping plaza that held a cute black owned business who sales custom picture frames and figurines. The shop was owned by Ruben and Eva Roberts. The cutest little couple who have owned that store since the late 1950s. The plaza itself though wasn't that old, but the couple bought the space and moved their store from downtown to this plaza to get a better flow of traffic. My parents have known them for years.

Since I am early for my date, I stop in to speak to them like I always do when I'm over this way. I walk in the store and immediately see Ms. Eva as she is dusting some of their newest pieces. "Lady Eva, how are you today."

She looks up and walks over to me, dropping the feather duster at the register. Before she reaches me, she opens her arms wide to gather me in them.

"Little Peace, how are you baby? It's been a month of Sundays since we've seen you."

"Lady Eva, I've been working. You know how it is. Sometimes you only have time to get to work and get home."

"Now child, don't bring me no mess like that. You can't work your life away. Then what will you have to look forward to?"

She squeezes me again and steps back, still leaving her hands on me. "Ruben, come on out here, Peace came to see you."

On cue, Mr. Ruben steps out from behind the curtain with wood dust on him. He dusts himself off as he walks towards me.

"There's my girl! What took you so long to come by here? We haven't seen you in a month of Sundays!"

I laugh because they always say the same things. "I've been working Mr. Ruben. A girl has to work to eat you know."

"Girl with a woman as fine as you? You don't have to work to eat. If you just let one of those men marry you, you'd be set for life. You know Junior is still trying to get your attention. That son of mine has been crazy about you since you two were in middle school. When are you going to settle down and get married? You're a good woman. Look at you all beautiful tonight. Where are you going looking like a freshly cooked steak and baked potato dinner?"

"I have a date Mr. Ruben. I'm meeting him at Theodosia's in a few minutes but I wanted to come by and get some Roberts loving before. Maybe what you both have will rub off on me and give me some luck tonight."

"Child, you don't need no luck. You need to be appreciated by a man who knows a good woman when he sees one. And the way these knuckle heads are around here, it's going to take a lot more than luck from an old marries couple for them to realize what a catch you are." Ms. Eva walks up to me and kisses my cheek. "Now gone over to that restaurant and meet that man and I pray that he has some sense and recognizes what he may have in you."

"Thank you both for the love and the encouragement. I'll be back soon to check on you two." I leave the store and wave again when I get outside before I walk over to the restaurant.

Instead of going inside, I sit on the veranda to wait for Shamar so that I can enjoy the summer breeze. Since I don't know what type of car he's driving, I sit patiently. To pass the time, I pull my cell out of my bag to look online to pass the time. I scroll through pages and then a shadow appears covering the sunlight that was blessing my melanin skin. I look up.

"Hello again Peace. So nice to see that you made it here safe and sound."

"And I return that comment back to you. And on time I see."

"Actually, I was early. I saw you pull up, walk across to that small shop, and then come back and sit down here. Are you ready to go in?"

"It's nice to see that a man respects the time of a woman. Yes, I'm ready to go in." He offers his hand to assist me to stand. I accept and rise from my seat.

"You look amazing. Very nice selection for dinner. That color looks amazing on you. Blue is definitely your color."

"Every color is my color." I correct him.

"Ok, that's something I'm going to have to see."

We walk into the restaurant and are shown to a booth. As we sit, the waiter appears and asks the usual questions and then gives us the specials for the night. We both order a glass of wine and the waiter leaves to fill our requests. While he is gone we review the menu and have small talk in between.

"Do you know what you would like to order?" he asks.

"Actually yes. I come here quit often."

"Of course you do. What are you having?"

"I'm having the Greek salad with the grilled salmon and potatoes on the side."

"That sounds good. But I think I'm going to have the lamb."

"Yes, the lamb here is absolutely delicious."

The waiter returns with the wine glasses and we place our order. Once the waiter walks away again, Shamar looks at me and asks. "Why is a beautiful woman like you single? You look to me to have your shit together and you my sista you are fine. It's hard to believe no one has snatched you up."

"I'm single by choice. I was involved with someone about six months ago and when it ended I decided to take some time for me. Nothing more than that."

"Get back to you huh? Sounds like it took a toll on you coming out of your last relationship."

"Not really. Before it ended, I knew it was headed down that path. It was just a matter of time really. So, when it happened, I was ready for it. But I still wanted to take the time to myself. You're actually the first date I've been on since."

"Well, I'm honored."

I laugh at the comment and look him in his eyes to see if I can read what's going on behind them. "And why are you single?"

"Kind of the same thing really. I was married and she walked out on me after 20 years. She was tired of me so she left."

"How long has it been since she left?"

"Six months." He drops eye contact with that comment and picks up his glass of wine. "Six months." He repeats.

"It's only been six months, you were married for 20 years, and you're already dating? Are you sure you're ready to be trolling the streets asking strangers on dates?"

"I asked you, didn't I? Shouldn't that answer your question?" He raises his eyes to look back at me.

That's when it hits me. Another man in transition from an event in his life. They always find me. I should have known.

Immediately, I know to keep my guard up because just like the rest, he won't stay. Now the only thing left is to figure out what my role in his life will be.

"That's a great response but how sure are you that it's true? Twenty years is a lifetime and to think that you're ready to date after how it ended is a little naïve. She left six months ago, but how long have you been divorced?"

"Oh, we're still technically married. The divorce hasn't been finalized just yet. We've been back and forth in court because of the marital property that we have and need to either dissolve or disperse equally."

"Which means technically, I'm on a date with a married man?"

"Technically, a legally separated man."

"Same thing in my book."

"If it means anything, I haven't seen her outside of the courtroom. We have nothing to say to each other. Our children are grown and I'm not fighting her on what she wants. We're just working out specifics really through the lawyers."

"Honestly, its none of my business. However, "separate" legal or otherwise is still married and I don't date married men or women."

"Wait, huh. Did you just add women to the end of that sentence?"

"Yes. I'm just being honest. I don't put myself in compromising positions on purpose and this seems like a compromising position. So, consider this our first and last dinner outing because it is NOT a date."

"Wow, you're a hard woman I see. I like that. I appreciate that you have morals and all, but this is really just an innocent dinner date. And it is a date because I asked you to come and I'm paying. In my book, that's a date."

"This is the first and the last." I smile and take a sip of my wine.

The waiter returns to take our order and disappears again. We have small talk about the weather and movies. I stay away from politics because I'm really not interested in that topic at all. He asks me what I do for a living and I return the question. For the remaining of the evening, we share decent conversation. It was an easy flow back and forth. Even during our meal, we continue to talk in between bites. The waiter returns once he notices our meals are finished and asks if we have room for dessert? We both decline and ask for the check.

"You know, I like the fact that when you talk and listen, you look me in the eyes. That must come from you being a lawyer huh? Not too many men do that these days. They look away when they talk so you can't see into their souls."

"I feel it's important to look someone in the eyes when you talk to them. It's a sign of respect. I want to know that you mean what you say and in return I want you to know I mean what I say."

"I can dig it." I say.

The waiter returns with the check. Shamar pulls out his wallet and hands his card to the waiter, never looking at the bill.

"I hope that wasn't to impress me."

"What do you mean Peace?"

"You didn't even look at the bill. You just handed your card to the waiter."

"Oh, no that wasn't to impress you beautiful, it's just what I always do. If I couldn't afford it, I wouldn't have asked you to dinner no matter where we decided to go." I smirk and sip the rest of my wine and wait for the waiter to return with the receipt and his card.

Five minutes later, we walk out of the restaurant and Shamar walks me to my car. I reach in my purse for my remote and he smoothly takes it from me to unlock my door so that he can open it. I smile on the inside and allow him to be a gentleman.

"Thank you for dinner. I enjoyed it." I say as he hands my keys back.

"You're welcome. I enjoyed it myself. It's nice to be out with a woman who can carry a full conversation. Sometimes, it's hard to find someone you can connect with so easily. We should do this again."

"Sounds good however not while you are still "separated" as you so eloquently put it. Once your divorce is final I'm sure we can do this again. But not until then." I get into my vehicle and Shamar closes the door. I start the car to roll down the window as I can tell he's still trying to talk to me.

"I understand. But to ask you out again, I need your phone number." He pulls out his phone and I give him my number. "I got you locked in. I'll text you later so that you have my number as well."

"You do that."

"Thank you again Peace. I hope to talk to you or even better see you soon."

"Enjoy the rest of your evening Shamar." I put my car in gear and pull out of the parking spot. I check the rearview mirror to see him still standing there watching the back of my car as it gets further and further away from him. Just as I reach the end of the row, I see him turn and walk in the direction of where I can only assume his car is located. I turn my music up in my car and prepare for my twenty-minute ride home. While sitting at the light on Shaffer Ave, my cell phone buzzes and the screen flashes indicating I just received a text message. I open my phone to read the message:

Hi Peace, it's Shamar. Just wanted to say again, thank you for accompanying me to dinner tonight. It was quite enjoyable.

Now you have my number. Have a safe drive home and I'll talk to you again soon.

I smile at the text and put my phone down. The light changes to green and I pull off turning the music up a little louder as I sing all the way home.

The Second Chance

"Girl, I'm so ready for a vacation. I haven't had one in a while."

"Camellia, you just went to Cali last month. If that wasn't a vacation what was it?"

"That was not vacation. That was James taking me to Cali for a weekend getaway. Shit, it's the least he could do after catching his car at his baby mama house when he told me he was going to him mama's. He knew he owed me and had to make sure it was good. I did way too much shopping on Rodeo. I tried to max out that damn black card." She laughs as we sit down for lunch in the breakroom.

"You're a mess Camellia. Do you think he learned his lesson?"

"Hell naw. I know he's still going to go over there and it's cool cuz I'll be over my baby daddy house at the same time. I ain't gone never stop dealing with him and he ain't gone never stop dealing with me. It's just the way it is. If you had kids you would understand."

"I'll take your word for it." I shake my head and begin to eat my lunch.

Don't get me wrong, Camellia is my girl. We've been cool since I started working here three years ago but I don't hold the same values as her and we don't come from the same background. She's so intelligent but she can't leave the hood mindset in the hood. She has a bright future and I only hope that the things she does outside of the office don't affect that.

"Alright now Peace, what's up with the dude you met a few months ago? Still haven't heard from him?"

"I told him not to contact me until his divorce was final and I meant that. He texted me a couple times but I didn't respond. I'm not getting into that type of situation again. Dating a married man is not the business. I'll never forget his face when I ran into him and his wife. His face dropped and I was immediately ashamed of myself for getting in that situation.

And she knew something wasn't right. She knew. She felt it. She was looking at my face and he was standing behind her shaking his head and mouthing "please don't". I was bent and I turned around and walked away. I heard her ask him did he know me and I heard him say, "no." That shit beat me down without a physical punch and I couldn't blame anyone but myself. And I knew better. My mother raised me better than that."

"We all make mistakes Peace. Trust me ain't nobody in this world perfect. We've all done something we're not proud of. And I know you learned from it."

"I know."

"Do you think you'll give dude another chance? I mean if he contacts you after his divorce is final?"

"Maybe, we had a good time. I just don't want to be a rebound. That shit is for the birds."

We continue eating our lunch and change the subject to people in the office and the upcoming annual company retreat. This year it's in Miami and bosses have booked five days full of conferences and training during the day and left us with the nights to ourselves. We enjoy our lunch for twenty more minutes and then go back to work.

When I open my office door, my cell phone rings. Being in no hurry to answer it I let it go to voicemail and sit at my computer. I read through the emails I received when I was at lunch and reply to a few. After 45 minutes, I pull my phone out of my purse to see who called. I notice I didn't have one missed call but five missed calls all from the same person, Shamar. He didn't leave a voicemail after any of the calls but he did send me a text message with a photo in between calls three and four.

You said you didn't want to hear from me

until my divorce was final. Look at the photo and

see that its final. Hit me back when you get a chance.

Do you like to bowl?

I smile at the added question on the end and then look at the attached picture. He was finally divorced. Now what? Do I respond or act like I haven't seen it? I decide to wait and not respond just yet. I need a little more time to think about it. I don't want this to be a repeat of what happens with me every time I get involved with someone. They find me, I fix them, and they move on. The first time it happened I was dating John the fireman, then it happened with Curtis the doctor, followed by Jessica the model, and most recently Rashaad the married one. All four of them were broken in one way or another and once I "fixed" them, they left me for someone else. And honestly, after each one, I got my heart broke. I went against my own better judgement and believed what they said and gave myself to them fully because I thought each of them was "The One" when we were together. But I was wrong.

For the rest of the day, I busy myself with work and time flies by. Next thing I know the clock on my desktop is saying it's 4:57pm. Time to shut it down and get out of here. It's Friday night and I'm ready to get home, light some candles, and take a long hot bath in my oversized tub. It's been a busy week and I deserve to have a large glass of wine and relax. I grab my purse, shut my office down, and head out the door. I join the rest of my co-workers at the elevator as we wait for the elevator to get to our floor. Finally, it reaches the eighth floor and the doors open. Before we can all get on, the people already on are coming off. I look at the faces of those exiting the elevator and realize one of them is Shamar. He smiles as we make eye contact.

"I thought I would catch you here." He smiles as he walks up to me and stops me from getting on the elevator.

"How do you know where I work?"

"I'm a corporate lawyer. I can find out anything I want just from one phone call. I know a lot of important people."

"Imagine that." I say with a smile.

"Did you see my text message and the attached document I sent with it?"

"I did."

"You told me not to contact you until it was final."

"I did."

"Well, it's final." His smile widens.

"I see."

"So, do you like to bowl?"

"As a matter of fact, I do."

"Well then Ms. Peace Willows, what do you say to a fun night of bowling? My treat of course." He pushes the button to call for the elevator.

"Sounds nice but I'm not really dressed for bowling."

"There is no dress code for bowling. You look great."

"Well, I've never seen anyone wearing a pants suit to a bowling alley. But if you'll like me go home and change I can meet you in about an hour and a half."

"You're not going to stand me up, are you?"

"If I say I'm going to be there, I'm going to be there. I am a woman of my word."

"Ok. I'll hold you to it then. I'll meet you in an hour and a half at Ball and Pins on Crest Lane." The elevator arrives and the door opens. Its empty besides us as we step on.

"I will be there."

We reach the underground parking garage where my car is parked. He walks me to my assigned space and again, takes my keys from me to unlock the doors. He opens my car door and I step in to get behind the wheel. Before he hands my keys back and closes the door, he says, "I'm not letting you get away from me Peace. You are what I have my eyes on. It's been that way since the first day I saw you."

"Well, you seem to be very determined to try and make that happen. I'm sure you're going to do all that you can to make that true."

"You're right. I am." He steps back and closes my door.

I smile and start my car. Shamar steps back and I ease out of my parking space toward the exit. He turns and heads back to the elevator.

An hour and a half later I pull up to the bowling alley. Out of the corner of my eye, I see Shamar get out of his car and walk up to mine. He opens my car door and I step out. He looks me over from my gray and blue Nikes to my blue tank top. He smiles at me as we walk toward the building. Being the gentleman that he is, he opens the door and allows me to walk through first as we meet with a member of the staff, get our shoes, and a lane. Bowling goes as you would expect. We have conversation in between frames and just enjoy each other's company. Everything flows effortlessly as we bowl three games.

"Do you want to bowl another round? I've beat you two out of three. I want to give you a chance to even the score." He says with a laugh.

"No, I think I'm good." I say and laugh as well.

"Ok. Is there anything else you would like to do? How about some dinner? It's Friday night. Or what about a movie? It's only 7:30pm."

"No. I think I've had enough fun for one night. It's been a long week and I just want to get some rest. I have some things planned for tomorrow. But thank you for the invitation."

"Are you sure? I would really like to spend some more time with you."

"I understand and I'm sure that you would but I really do need to get some rest."

"Alright, well I tried. But I see that you are not going to make this easy. That's alright, I'm always up for a challenge."

We sit down and change back into our shoes. I can tell he's trying to stall but my mind is not going to change. I had planned on going home and resting tonight and that is where I'm headed. But I have to admit that this was fun. We talk a little more as we walk back to the shoe return and Shamar pays for our games and we leave the bowling alley. He walks me to my car and in Shamar fashion, he takes my keys, opens the door, returns my keys, and I get it. I start my car, close the door, and put the window down.

"Thank you for today. It was fun."

"You're welcome Peace. I enjoyed myself too. I wish you would let me take you to dinner though. I'm not ready to let you go just yet."

"Yeah, but we can't always get what we want."

"Ok. Well, I'll hit you up tomorrow and if you have time for me, then maybe we can get together."

"Maybe. Enjoy he remainder of your night Shamar."

"You do the same Peace."

I shift my car into gear and pull out of the parking lot, once again leaving Shamar standing there. And as it seems to be his way, he watches my car until I am out of sight. I laugh to myself. This man must be on a mission and I am definitely the prize he is trying to win.

The Courtship

For the past three months, I have to admit that Shamar has been very persistent in his want to date me. I'm not sure if it's because I am making him work for it or because he is really that interested. Either way, it's cute but I'm still going to remain cautious with him. I know how it goes when someone is in transition from one life experience and moving on to the next. Sometimes their need to continue on with life is not as immediate as they think and they don't give themselves enough time to heal from the previous one. The need to get back to what they had and that companionship has a stronger pull than people think. As he continues to text me daily, I do my best to keep that in mind.

During the first month of dating, we took time to get to know what each other liked. We went to dinner, movies, bowling, and anything else we could find to spend quality time with each other. We shared long late-night conversations when we apart and made sure that we said goodnight every night even if through text. I couldn't imagine what would make his ex-wife leave him and he never really shared that information with me. In our second month of dating, he invited me over to his home where he cooked me dinner and we sat in his tv room and watched movies until late into the night. He asked me to stay but I wasn't ready and he understood. It felt nice to know that I was dating someone who respected my decisions.

He's been very patient in my choice not to be intimate with him. He hasn't pressed me about it and I'm not sure if it's because he has someone he's seeing other than me. And if that's the case, then that is truly his business. I have told him several times that I have no ties to him nor him to me. But he has told me that he is a man, who can only do one thing at a time. And that is because he wants to put his energy into that one thing once he decides it's something that he truly wants. Up until this point, I hadn't believed him. But he has shown me that his word is his bond.

As I pick out my outfit for the night, I decide to choose something a little different. A little sexier than what I would normally wear for a movie and dinner date. That's because I have made the decision that tonight was the night that we would be intimate for the first time. Thus far, all we've done is kiss at the end of the night. Nothing more. Tonight though, that is going to change. I pick out a red and black off the shoulder dress with red stiletto shoes. I view my reflection in my mirror and approve of the final outcome. My text message notification rings.

Hey Doll. Be there in 10 mins. Can't wait to see you.

I smile and type my response.

Ok. I'm almost ready.

Looking in the mirror, I smile again, grab some perfume and spray just a little on. Take one more look and go downstairs to wait for him to arrive. In ten minutes, the doorbell rings and I find myself almost running to open the door for him. As I pull the door open, the look on his face speaks silent volumes. His lips part just a little to show that he approves and his smile gets a wide as the Cheshire cat from Alice in Wonderland. I step back and he opens the screen door with a dozen white roses in hand and steps into the house.

"Damn woman, you look good."

"Thank you. I do what I can on a Saturday."

"Well you have outdone yourself tonight." He hands me the roses and steps closer for an embrace. He squeezes me tight and smells my neck. "And you smell like candy."

I giggle like a little school girl and walk toward the kitchen so that I can put the flowers in a vase. While he walks behind me, I can feel his eyes on my behind as it sways with each step I take. I smile as I catch his reflection in the kitchen window as I put water in the vase.

"Can you unwrap the roses so I can put them in the vase?"

"Of course Doll, I was already doing that."

"Thank you." I turn back to see him standing there with the roses in hand waiting to place them in the vase. I set the vase down and he places the roses in and does a slight adjustment of the arrangement. We lock eyes and I smile again. "Let me place these on the coffee table and then we can go." I place the vase in the front room and step back to view the scene. I love when he brings me flowers.

"You ready Doll?" he had started calling me Doll after dating for a month. I asked him why after the first few times and he said, 'because that's what you look like and that's how you should be treated.'

"Yes." I pick up my purse and keys from the sofa table and we head out. "Are we going to the movies first or to dinner?"

"Dinner. I made reservations for us at La Joie down in the district. Something different. How is that?" He opens the car door for me to get in and then goes around the car to get in himself.

"Sounds good. I haven't had French cuisine in a long time. They opened that restaurant a few months ago right?" I say after he is seated and starts the car. We back out of the driveway to get our date officially started.

"Yes, my brother and his wife own it. I've been waiting to take you because I wanted you to meet them. He's not my biological brother but I've known him my entire life. Thick as thieves in every way. His name is Greg and his wife is Shanell. They lived in Paris for three years where she was a chef and he worked for this international investment company. They moved back to the states two years ago and this was her dream. And my brother made it happen."

"That's amazing. Are you sure you're ready for me to meet your friends? We haven't been dating that long."

"I got this Doll. If I wasn't sure, I wouldn't do it."

"Ok." I settle back in the car and we listen to music as he drives through the city to our destination. Out the corner of my eye I watch him drive and bounce his head to the music. He places his right hand on my left knee and I turn my head to look out the window. I smile and I feel the goosebumps on my arm raise from his touch. I wonder if he can see them?

As he pulls into the downtown district, he lowers the volume on the music and turns his head to me. "You ok? You've been quiet since we left your house."

"Yes, I'm fine. Was enjoying the music and your and on my knee."

"You sure? If you're not ready to meet them, we can go somewhere else."

"I'm ready if you are. Besides, I'm really interested to see you interact with your people. I want to see the real you."

"I'm always the real me Doll. What you see is what you get."

"We'll see." I say and smile.

He pulls into the small parking lot for the restaurant and find a parking space. He turns he car off, gets out, and walks around to open the door on my side. Helping me out of the car, we proceed to the front of the restaurant where he opens the door for me to enter. We are immediately met by a brown skinned man, about the same height as Shamar, and he looked to be around the same age. They do the brother man handshake and pull each other into an embrace. This must be Greg. When they part, Greg looks over Shamar's shoulder at me. Stepping to the side Shamar makes the introductions.

"Greg, this is my lady, Peace Willows. Peace, this is my brother, Greg Johnson." Greg steps forward to shake my hand.

"Nice to meet you Peace."

"Likewise." I say.

"Yeah bruh, I see what you were talking about." Greg says to Shamar and they both smile.

"And what does that mean?" I ask them both.

"Nothing bad, nothing bad at all. It's nice to finally meet you. That's all." Greg smiled and looked at Shamar again.

"I don't believe that at all but I'll let it slide this time."

"I have your table ready for you. Follow me."

I walk ahead of Shamar behind Greg to the table. As we go through the restaurant, I admire the décor and design. I have never been to Paris but being in this restaurant definitely makes me feel like I'm there now. Instead of music over the intercom, there is a string quartet playing in the center of the restaurant for all the patrons to enjoy. Even with the music, the individual conversations held at the private table are not loud. The artwork and lighting are perfect and could have been right out of a movie scene filmed in Paris. We reach our table and Shamar pulls out my chair for me to sit. He and Greg share a few quiet words and then he takes his seat.

"If you need anything, please have the server come find me. I'll let Shanell know that you're here. I'm sure she'll come out after a while to see you herself and meet you Peace. I'll come back by later. Please enjoy yourselves." He smiles and walks off to greet other patrons.

"That's Greg." Shamar says after Greg walks away. He smiles at me.

51

"I see. Seems like a nice guy. You two are really close. I can tell from the way you interact with each other."

"Yes, we are. We've been through the a few storms together and always made it out with most of the skin on our backs. From elementary school through college, we've had each other's backs. We've never let anyone come in between us. Never had a fight. Never had a fallout. It's rare to find someone like that these days. He's my brother through and through. Blood couldn't make us any closer."

"I can tell. That's great to have someone in your corner like that. Not a lot of people are that lucky."

"True. True."

We open our menus and wait for the server to appear. On cue, she comes over and gives us the specials for the night and suggests the house wine to accompany our meals. We each order a glass of wine and ask for a little more time to make a decision on our meals. She walks off and we continue to try and make a selection. I glance up to see a woman coming towards us in a chef's hat and apron. We make eye contact and I instantly know that this must be Shanell. She approaches the table and taps Shamar on his shoulder.

"Hey brother. How are you?"

He stands to greet her with a hug. "Hey sis. Look at you! You look great and completely in your element." He hugs her again and then steps back.

"Awe, thank you. Please sit down. And who is this beautiful woman? You must be Peace."

"Shanell, you are correct. This is my lady, Peace. Peace, this is my sister Shanell."

She extends her hand and I do the same. "Hello. Your restaurant is absolutely beautiful. It has all the ambiance of Paris."

"Thank you and it's nice to finally meet you. My brother has been talking about you non-stop. You have him smiling like I haven't seen him smile in a long time. And thank you. This is my baby. I've wanted to have my own restaurant for a long time. I'm just blessed to be able to see my dream come to life. Have you ever been to Paris?"

"Well, the smile is truly two-fold. It's nice to know that he is saying good things about me. Oh, no, I've never been to Paris. I hope to go one day. And if it's half as beautiful as I've seen in movies along with the details you've put in here, I will probably never come back." I laugh.

"It is one hundred times as beautiful in person. I hope you get to go one day." She smiles at me and then turns back to Shamar.

"Ok, brother. I have to get back to the kitchen. If I may make a suggestion on dinner. Try the Chicken Basquaise. I make it with a special homemade wine sauce that is amazing. Or the Steak Diane laced with brandy. Honey, you will not be dissatisfied."

"Thanks sis."

"Alright, you two enjoy your night. And come by the house next week Shamar, there are some things there for you that Jessica brought by."

I saw Shamar look at me when she said Jessica's name but I did not allow my face to change in any way.

"Ok. Thanks, I will."

She says her good-byes and walks back in the direction to which she appeared from initially.

"Sorry about that. I didn't know she would mention Jessica's name."

"No, it's ok. You can't know everything that everyone is going to say. Don't worry about it."

We let the mention of his ex-wife's name go and continue on with our date. The server finally returns and we take Shanell's advice. I order the chicken and he orders the steak. We have small conversation as we wait for our dinner and somewhere throughout this conversation, we begin to hold hands. Once our entrees arrive, we bless the food and begin to eat. The food is amazing and we continue our small talk throughout the meal.

It occurs to me that our conversations are not limited to one area. We talk about everything without fear or judgement. The only topic that we seem to stay away from is politics. Mostly because I'm not a fan of politics at all. But all other areas are open for discussion. I've never known a man or dated a man that I could be so open with. It is refreshing to say the least.

We finish our meals and the server clears the table. She asks if we would like dessert and we decline. He checks his watch and we change the subject to selecting a movie to go see.

"Honestly, I'd rather sit here for a little while longer and then go back to my house." The look in my eyes changes and he catches the hint. He stares at my face and into my eyes so deeply, I can feel it piercing through me.

"Are you sure? I'm not in a hurry Doll." He places his hand on mine.

"I'm sure. I've been thinking about it and I think it's time."

"Let's see how the rest of the night goes. If you change your mind, it's ok."

I shake my head and we sit another half an hour enjoying the atmosphere and the conversation. The server returns with the check and before she can walk off Shamar hands his credit card to her without looking at the bill. She takes the card and goes to the back where the registers are located. She returns after five minutes and Shamar signs the receipt. On cue, Greg returns to the table to walk us out. At the front door, the again embrace and share some words quietly.

"Peace, it was great to finally meet you. I hope you enjoyed our little place here. Please come back anytime."

"Thank you. It was nice meeting you and your wife as well. I will definitely return and please let Shanell know the Chicken Basquaise was delicious."

"I will let her know." he turns to Shamar. "Alright bruh, you be safe tonight. We can chop it up later."

"No doubt bruh. And again, the place is beautiful. Congratulations."

"Thanks man. Have a great night."

We walk out the door and make our way to the car. Shamar drives in the direction of my house and again we ride through the city listening to the music on his iPod. When we reach my neighborhood, I feel my stomach start to flutter. My nerves have kicked in like a school girl with her first crush considering having sex for the first time. It's not that I am afraid but nervous all the same. He looks over at me and places his hand on my knee again. My body relaxes and I look at his hand. We pull in the driveway and make our way into the house.

I slip my shoes off and walk to the tv room where he sits on the sofa and turns on the television. I sit next to him as he finds a movie to watch.

"We don't have to do anything Doll. It's no hurry. I enjoy spending time with you. We have time." He places his arm around me and pulls me close placing a kiss on my neck.

"I'm going to change into some shorts. If you want anything, help yourself."

"Ok. I'll make some popcorn for the movie."

I go to my room and pull out a change of clothes. I grab a pair of shorts and a tank top. Before changing, I take a quick shower and take off all my make-up and jewelry. I decide not to put on any underwear just the shorts and the tank top. When I return to the tv room, Shamar has loosened up a little and taken off his shoes. I sit next to him and he hands me the bowl of popcorn. We watch the movie he's selected, laughing at the funny parts and looking at each other at the parts we both know are ridiculous.

The movie ends and we look at each other. I decide it's now or never and lean in to kiss him. His response is what I expected. Unrushed and soft. Subtle and intimate. The touch of his hands on my body gave me shivers and that's when I knew for sure that now was the right time. Once our kiss breaks, I rise up from the sofa and grab his hand leading him to the room he's never seen to experience a night like he's never had.

We enter the dimly lit room and he stops. Looking around at the room, he seems to be memorizing what it looks like in case he doesn't get the chance to ever see it again. I give a tug to his hand and lead him over to the bed. He undresses me gently and takes in the full picture of my body. Then I return the favor. We climb onto my king-sized bed and take our time exploring each other. No words are spoken between us. There's no need for any. We share this time with each other the way we want to. Uninhabited but tender. Soft kisses and moans. We tenderly touch each other and live in this moment. Nothing matters outside of this room right now and we make it all about us. He is everything I hoped he would be and I am exactly what he needs me to be. The energy is magnetic and we relish every second we have together at this time. And when it's over, we lay in each other's arms. Still quiet as we think about what we just shared, until we both slip off to sleep.

****

It's been six months and this has been the best six months of my life. I never knew that I could be this happy. To be completely honest about the whole thing, I told him about my theory of me being the "Transitional Woman" and how it has played out for me in the past. I explained to him how I forever find myself in the situation of being the woman who has helped someone get through a time in their life, only for them to leave me in the end, and then the next person they commit themselves to becomes the one they marry or build a life with.

His response is always, "You are no one's transitional woman and I don't want to hear that from you again. You are not my transitional woman. You are my woman." By now, I believe him and I trust him. I trust him with my heart. And he trusts me with his. Last night, when we were getting off of the phone, he ended our conversation with, "Love you, good night" and he hung up. I was so in shock I didn't know what to do. Whether to call him back, text him, or act like I didn't hear him. I know for sure though, I need to decide how I feel.

"I love him." I say out loud. That's the first time I've said it and I know it to be true. Am I in love with him? That's a question I really need to ask myself. And in reality, I've never truly been in love with someone so how would I know if I am or not? But for now, I am sure that I love him.

Sometimes it feels like everything has been a blur. The time we've spent together has increased and he's introduced me to his family. The initial resistance from some members was a little heavy at times but once they actually sat down and had a conversation with me, things smoothed themselves out. Thankfully. Overall, I can tell they are really good people with good intentions, just a little rough on the outside.

As far as my side of the family, there's not many of us left. We're a small group who are pretty wide spread. But he and I plan to attend this year's family reunion to give him a chance to see where I come from. That will definitely be an interesting trip because my family although small makes a big impression.

****

Ten months in and we are still going strong. Who would have thought that bumping into someone at the bookstore would turn into all that this has become? My smile is brighter and it's evident that there is some true happiness in my life. My heart skips a beat when I think about him and all that he is to me. I have come to not only love this man for who he is from my heart. I love him from my spirit. And that is something I have never felt before. My spirit aches for him, it longs for him. I have come to trust that this man is my soulmate. The one I was made for. When I think of him, I instantly smile. I dream about him. I pray for him.

There was never a point in my life where I truly thought this was going to be possible for someone like me. Someone who was broken from events long before this time. It was in my heart that no one would be able to see past my faults. And because of that, I had succumbed to the realization that I was stuck in the perpetual cycle of being the forever transitional woman only capable of helping others. Leaving nothing for myself. But he changed all of that in my eyes and in my heart. I'm still in awe that this happened but I am so elated that it has.

How did I get so lucky? The future has changed for me and I am walking into it with a smile on my face, a good man by my side, and the promise of beautiful days.

The Heart Changes

This week makes one year I've been dating Shamar. I have some things planned for the weekend to celebrate as a surprise. All week I've been thinking about seeing Shamar. Not in the normal sense as I do every week, in a more intense way. All the time that we spend on the phone and hanging out has been amazing. During the time that we've been dating, we've had some disagreements which is normal but nothing detrimental to our growth as a couple. But lately, I've noticed a difference in him. There's something going on with him but he hasn't shared it with me yet. I won't pressure him to share it with me either. He always does things in his time and I respect that.

As I get ready for our normal date night, I hear my phone buzz signaling a text message has come across. I pick up my phone and read:

Hey Doll. Omw. Be there shortly.

I text back to let him know I received it.

Ok luv, see you soon. Drive safely.

I place my phone back on my bed and continue my ritual of getting pretty for him. I'm sure we'll talk tonight during dinner. I just want to tell him that I'm here if he needs anything. Reassure him that what we have is solid and real. Tell him that I have his back no matter what.

The music is playing as I finish putting on my dress for dinner. I check the bedside clock and it reads 7:15pm which meant that he will be pulling up soon. I check myself in the full-length mirror in my bedroom and smooth my red off the shoulder dress down in the front. I do a full turn in the mirror, step up and check my make-up. "Girl, you look damn good."

I hear his car in the drive-way and as usual wait to hear the doorbell ring before I go to it. Once I hear the chime, I head down the stairs, take a deep breath, and open the door. The smile on my face fades as I look into his eyes and step back so that he can enter.

"Hi." I step into him to hug him and he places one arm around me, then kisses my cheek.

"We need to talk." Shamar says while stepping into the house after I open the door for him.

Of course, we all know what that means. No matter who says it. It always carries the implications of something bad. Every relationship movie and romance novel has given us that backstory.

"We need to talk? Ok." I say and walk into the living room and sit down. "Let's talk."

He sits next to me and grabs my hand. He hasn't made eye contact with me since he walked in the house and I can tell he's taking deep breaths. He doesn't say anything for a few minutes which makes it worse. The tension is building and I can feel my own breathing change.

"What is it Shamar?"

Still looking at our hands intertwined and not looking in my face he takes a deep breath and then looks at me. I see the tears in his eyes and feel my heart drop. "Peace, you know that this last year has meant a lot to me. I have grown to love you in a way I never thought I would be able to love another woman after my divorce from Jessica. You have changed how I see myself and helped me through the roughest year of my life. I know how lucky I am to have bumped into you and how much better my life is that you finally gave me a chance."

I look at him and feel the tears in my own eyes begin to form but I force them back because I can't give him the pleasure of seeing me cry or get emotional in that way. I want to say something but no words are forming. My brain is shutting down and my heart is taking over and I can't breathe.

"I've been thinking about this for a while and I wasn't quite sure if what I was feeling was real. I put some distance between us for the last few weeks to see if it was just my nerves or if it was my heart. And I've come to realize that it's my heart. You are a wonderful woman who has so much to offer. You are young, beautiful, and successful and any man who is with you is the luckiest man on earth. But right now, that man is not me. I love you Peace but I'm not in love with you. My heart is not in a place where I can give it to you the way you deserve. I want that for you and I don't know when I'll ever be able to do that. I can't let you or ask you to wait for me to figure out if or when I'll ever be ready for that."

I snatch my hand away from him and stand up from the sofa. I walk to the other side of the room to put some space in between us because my first instinct is to slap him. My breathing become shallow and I close my eyes. "What? What? Wait…. What?" I shake my head from side to side trying to not hear what I am so obviously hearing. Trying to not process this scene.

"I'm sorry. I'm so sorry."

"Wait. You come to my house like everything is all good. I've talked to you all week and you never gave me any inclination that you were going to have this talk with me or that you were feeling this way. As a matter of fact, you say you've been feeling this way for a while, and you never said anything. You let me walk around here thinking that everything between us was good. And now you come over here and tell me that you don't want to see me anymore because you're not in love with me …. but you love me."

"I'm sorry." He rises from the sofa and walks toward me. I walk away to maintain the space between us as my mind tries to process this entire conversation.

"What? How long have you been feeling like this?" I walk from room to room and he continues to follow me through my house. As I walk through the kitchen, I see him out the side of my eye watch me to see if I'm going toward the knives. But that is the last thing on my mind. I'm trying to process and stay

70

calm and process and nothing is working. My brain is not firing on all cylinders at all.

"Honestly, about two months." He whispers. "Please stop walking, stand still."

"I can't stand still. I'm trying to process what you're saying and you have to let me do that."

"Please stop walking away from me. Bae..."

"Don't call me that! You don't have the right to call me that. And I'm walking away because I don't want you to touch me." My heart is racing while my mind is shutting down.

"I'm sorry but I needed to be honest with you. You deserve that. Please stop walking, I won't touch you."

"So, you come to my house to tell me this? You come to my house, my place of peace, and you tell me this?" I feel like everything is going black as I try to continue to function but my body is doing whatever it wants to do right now.

"Would you rather I have told you over the phone or through a text message?"

"I'd rather we met at a neutral place that held no significance in my life or our relationship. A place that I would never go to again. A place where that memory would have stayed. Not the place where I lay my head every night. The place that I come to for peace and solitude. The place that holds so many good memories for us." Was he trying to be smart with that comment? It's taking everything in me to not jump on him right now.

He drops his head and puts his hands in his pockets. I look at him and can tell he doesn't know what to say. He shuffles his feet back and forth in place and avoids eye contact with me. I stare at him as I feel my heart break and crumble in my chest. What else is there to say?

"Peace, I didn't want to keep this going with you when I knew my heart was feeling this way. What would you have rather me do? Continue seeing you so that I can sleep with you and let you think that everything was ok? You deserve better

72

than that. And right now, I can't give you more. I can't give you what you want. I have some things that I need to take care of and they are a priority for me. Putting that together with the feelings in my heart, it's not fair for me to put you in that position. You deserve someone who has the time for you. Someone who has the ability to love you the way you need and deserve. The way I wish I could. I really want that for you. My heart wants that for you."

"Your heart wants that for me? Are you serious? Did you really just say that? My heart wants that for me too and my heart is saying that it wants that with you." I can hear him but I'm not processing everything that he says. Some of the conversation is sounding like the teacher from the Charlie Brown cartoons. I open my mouth to speak these final words to him but don't raise my eyes to look at him. "You know, I thank you for being honest with me. I thank you for not using me. You can go. You can go now."

"I'm sorry Peace. I …"

"I said, you can go. Now." I turn my back as he takes one step towards me then changes his mind. He turns away from me and walks to my front door. I hear the door open and then I hear it close behind him. I hold myself back from running to the window or the door to stop him or watch him pull off. All I can do is stand there and try to breathe. That's all my body will allow me to do.

I hear the car start and the sounds of him backing out of my driveway. And then there was silence and I knew that Shamar, the man I come to know, was gone. And with him, he took my heart in a way that no one has ever taken my heart before. Because no one has ever had it before him.

I let myself get wrapped up in this man in a way that I had never done previously. After a certain point, I had come to believe that this was not another transitional woman experience but the real deal. I thought my days as the transitional woman was over because a man had found me who loved me, who told me loved me, who showed me he loved me, and treated me like he loved me. How did I miss it? How did I get it wrong? How did I let him in? Why is it that I could not see that this was just another time where someone came into my life just for me to fix them and for them to walk away?

Lost in my own emotions I had to take a leave of absence from work. It's been three weeks now and even though we had only been involved for a year it felt like a lifetime. I've never been this broken after the end of any relationship. No matter what I do, I can't seem to stop crying and pick myself up to keep moving. There's no answer that anyone can give me. No consolation that anyone can provide me with. I've been praying for relief and praying for strength and still here I am, in my pajamas in my bed with tear stained pillows and crust in my eyes.

I've turned off my phone, ignored the knocks on the door, and let the mail pile up inside the box. My car hasn't moved this entire time and to be honest, I haven't eaten more than three of four crackers a day. I know this is not healthy but I can't find the energy to do anything. I'm sure I've lost at least 10 pounds because I'm not taking care of myself. Every day I wake up and wish my mother was alive so I could call her and ask her what to do. But she's not. She went to be with the Lord eight years ago. I lay here thinking, "what would mama say to pull me out of this mood and get me back up and moving?" but my brain is not functioning. I can't even hear her voice in my head.

"How did I let this man break me?" I say out loud as tears roll down my face. I roll over and cry myself to sleep.

The television wakes me up. I look at the bedside clock and see it's 2:30am. I haven't eaten anything and my body is telling me to go use the bathroom. I walk past my floor length mirror at glance at myself. Disappointed in what I look like, I continue to the bathroom to relieve myself. I sit down and out of nowhere I begin to cry. By now I would have thought I was out of tears but no, I'm not. They stream down my face in silence as I remember every date, every kiss, every time we made love. The memories won't stop and with each tear that drops, I see in my mind's eye his face, his smile, his eyes. I hear his laugh and feel the way his hand would hold mine, touch my body, and pull me in close.

I grab some tissues and wipe my face. After blowing my nose, I finish using the bathroom and wash my hands. My stomach is empty but I have no appetite. I check the cracker packet on the beside nightstand to find nothing but crumbs. Picking up my phone and turning it on, I walk to the kitchen for something to put into my body. Have you ever had the moment you feel like your body is about to shut down because you are not taking care of it? That's what my body is going through right now and I know I need to put something more in it than crackers. My phone turns on and immediately the text messages and voicemail notifications received begin to load. After four minutes, the phone is quiet and I pick it up to scroll through the texts. There's several texts from Mila and Camellia both asking the same things. If I was ok, did I need anything, they're worried about me. Camellia even texted that she came by the house every day for a week but I didn't answer the door for her. Her last text said that if she didn't hear from me within 24 hours that she would call the local police to break down my front door to make sure I was still alive. But no texts from Shamar. I call the voicemail and the recording says I have twenty messages. I hang up because I know I'm not in the mindset to listen to them right now and I know that Shamar's voice will not be on the other line checking on me. I start to cry again. I sit at the counter stool and put my head in my hands as the endless tears seemingly run down my face creating a puddle on the countertop. I keep my eyes closed because opening them now would only make me relive the reality of not seeing his name with a text in my phone.

Does he even care? Is he missing me? Did I ever mean anything to him? All questions that I can't answer and in reality, questions I don't want to know the answers to. Why? Because if he answers are not what I want it to be, it would only break me more. I feel like I'm left with nothing. That I'm not worthy of being loved and this is just another case of being thrown away.

Because that's what the transitional woman is? In reality, she is the woman that no one really wants. She is the woman that is only good for one thing. Not long-term love but short-term lust. Just good enough to be dealt with during the transition from one stage in life to the other. I just thought this time was different. I thought that he was different, that us together was different.

Not only did I lose my love but I lost my best friend. My best friend, my confidant, my heart, the one who I felt was my soulmate. It finally hit me that he was so much more to me than any other person I had dealt with who was in transition for whatever reason. Why? Because I was able to just be me with him. Just me no pretending to be, no expectations or requirements. Just me. He didn't need or ask for anything more than that. He just wanted me. Or so I thought. He was the first person I talked to in the morning and the last voice I heard at night. And now that is gone and I don't know how to handle it.

I forgo the food and head back to bed. I don't even know what day it is and at this point, I don't want it to be any day. I don't want to feel anything. I just want to sleep because I don't know what's going on when I'm sleep. In my room, I grab the bottle of sleeping pills next to my bed and pour five of them in my hands. Even in the dark, I can see the yellow pills in my palm. They look like tic-tacs but I know they're not. What they are, are my escape from this world and this pain. Maybe a permanent escape...maybe temporary. At this point, do I really care? I just want to escape. Will anyone really miss me? Will anyone really care? Will anyone even know? I raise the pills to my mouth and grab the water bottle by my bed.

"Wait. This is not the way. This is not what I see in you. This is not you." Is what I heard right before I put those pills in my mouth. I know no one is in my room with me. I drop my hand and close my eyes. "Don't do this." I hear it. But the pain is so heavy on me. The loss is so deep in my soul.

"You told me, to bring my deepest desires and needs to you and leave them at your feet. You told me to trust you and you will provide. You told me that I could rely on your word and your ways and your promise and that you would always be there and take of me. I did that! I DID THAT! And this is what I got! WHY?! I did what you said and this is what I got in return! WWWHHHYYYYYY! YOU TOLD ME TO TRUST YOU! I love this man from my spirit. I pray for me him more than I pray for me. I dream of him. I tell my friends and family about him. I saw my future with him. But again, this turns out to be the same as every other time. The same as every other person. I felt this one was different. It was different. He was supposed to be the one. I GAVE THIS TO YOU AND YOU WERE SUPPOSED TO TAKE CARE OF ME AND MY HEART! YOU TOLD ME TO TRUST YOU!" I scream into the atmosphere as more tears endlessly stream from my eyes. My heart aches as I wish for him. My heart breaks because I know he's not coming back. My spirit is broken and I don't know how to fix it. I fall to my knees as my head rests on the bed. Then I hear it.

"It's not for you to fix. It's for you to trust in me. To know that I will never and have never left you alone. When are you going to realize that you did not put your love in that man. You put your love in Me and I am still here. I have not left you.

What I wanted you to see is that no matter what happens, I am still here and I know what you really want, no matter what you have said to others. You are not the transitional woman. You are a woman of my making and this is just a test. I am preparing you. You have nothing to worry about. You were not ready for all that it was and even though you were happy, you weren't fully fulfilled. I had to show you that there is something coming for you that you are not expecting and it will be all that you want it to be. It will be. It will be the starting point for your newest and most profound journey. Do not fear and do not turn away. All that you have been through with each relationship, no matter the length, was to prepare you for this. It's getting you ready for what I have in store for you. Your strength is boundless. Your heart is healed. Your spirit is restored. Hear my voice and know that I am here. Keep your trust and faith in me. I am here, I never left. You had to go through this to prepare you for what is coming. Cry it out this last time and breathe in your renewed air to go with your renewed heart. Because I'm coming for you. I'm coming for that smile and that laugh and that beautiful soul of yours. Prepare, wait, and have patience. Now sleep without those pills and you will wake up refreshed and ready to begin your process of healing. Know that your love is not taken lightly in my eyes and I see you. You are not alone."

I look at the pills in my hand. Did I just hear what I think I heard? Could it be? Is it my mind playing tricks on me? Do I trust that this was a message? I throw the pills in the trash, climb into my bed, and close my eyes. Sleep immediately takes me over. Let my healing begin.

After It All- 3 Years Later

It's a beautiful Sunday afternoon and I have my soul music playing in the background as I prep for my Sunday dinner. My cell phone rings and I look at the screen to see it's a number I don't have saved in my contacts and against my better judgement, I answer it anyway.

"Hello."

"Hello." A man's voice replies. "May I speak to Peace?"

"Speaking." I acknowledge.

"How are you?" he says.

"I'm well. May I ask who's calling because you obviously know who I am."

"You don't remember my voice?"

"I'm sorry, I don't. Is there a reason I should?"

"I was hoping you would. This is Gregory Johnson, I'm a friend of Shamar Michaels."

Wow, Shamar Michaels. I hadn't heard that name in years. "Oh yes, hi Greg, how are you?"

"I'm good, very good in fact. But I'm not calling to talk to you about me. I was calling to talk to you about Shamar. I know you two have not been in contact for a few years, and I'm actually surprised I was able to reach you at this number. But I have something I wanted to say to you."

"Well Greg you're right. I haven't had any contact with Shamar in about three years now. I hope that things are ok with him but I'm really not sure why you would be calling me with anything to say about him. We dissolved our relationship a long time ago. I'm sure by now that Shamar has moved on with his life beyond what we had."

"Peace, you are still so outspoken and quick to reply. Let me finish. I'm calling you because I was asked to by Shamar.

He gave me your number with the hopes that it was still the same. He asked me to contact you because he wanted to reach out to you himself but was not sure what your reaction would be."

"Ok, so now after three years, he asked you to reach out to me for what exactly? Like I said, we dissolved our relationship long ago."

"You know that old saying, 'If you love someone set them free. If they come back they're yours; if they don't they never were.' Well…"

As I start to say something smart when he began spewing that quote of nonsense, my doorbell rings. Thinking nothing of this occurrence, I walk to the front door and open the door to see no one there but when I step forward to view the right and left side, out steps Shamar with baby blue and pink colored roses in his hand and a smile of hope on his face and in his eyes. I raise my right hand to my mouth to cover it as I stand there in shock. I look past Shamar to see Greg standing in my driveway with his cell phone still to his ear and a smile on his face. He hangs up the phone as if to say, "My job here is done," gets into his car, and backs out.

I look back to Shamar, "What are you doing here?"

"I was wondering if you would like to go bowling?" I can see the glimmer of hope in his eyes as he asks the question. They scream "please" in silence.

"What?" I ask totally bewildered and caught off guard.

"I was wondering if you would like to go bowling? You do bowl still, don't you?"

"What are you doing here? You show up on my doorstep after three years and ask me if I want to go bowling, really? You cannot be serious?"

"I am. Dead serious in fact. So, I ask you again, Peace Willows, would you like to go bowling with me?"

"No." I say and step back to close my door.

"Woman, are you honestly going to close the door in my face? Do you know what I had to go through to find you!? Even with the same phone number, you do not live in the same place you lived three years ago. You do not work in the same location you worked three years ago and I know because I went there last week looking for you. As a matter of fact, to ask you the same question only with white roses that time. Are you not at least happy to see me? Have you not wondered how I've been and if I was even ok?"

I open the door again and step up close to my screen door to make sure that what I had to say was clear and understood. "It is not my concern what you had to go through to find me. Why? Because you had every opportunity three years ago to make sure that I never walked away from you. You had every chance to make us work. You had every opportunity to show me how much I meant to you. But you didn't, did you? I remember it like it was yesterday. I've relived repeatedly in my head and dreams, it always ends the same. You telling me that you weren't ready. You were lost. And you didn't want to hold me back from being found by a man who would love me the way I deserved. Love me the way you only wish you could have. Now you show up on my doorstep with roses and a smile and an offer to go bowling? This has to be some kind of joke to you. Get your ass off my porch and leave me alone. You didn't want me then and I don't want you now."

"Peace, please give me a minute. That's all I ask. May I come in? It's Sunday afternoon, so I know you're in that kitchen prepping for your Sunday dinner. While you get your food ready, I'll talk. If you don't like what I have to say, I'll leave and never bother you again."

I look in his face and see the sincerity in his eyes. Against my better judgement, I push open the screen door from my side and signal for him to enter as he asked. He accepts the gesture and grabs the handle of the door. I turn to walk back to my kitchen. In my heart, I have no true intentions on listening to anything that he has to say but this is the only way that I can get him to leave without making a scene on my front yard where my neighbors will see.

In the kitchen, I step back up to the island to continue prepping my vegetables for the stir-fry. He sits at one of the barstools after replacing the tulips in the large glass vase on my kitchen table with the roses he brought.

"I know this was unexpected and I know you hate for people to pop up at your house. But I also know that if I had done this any other kind of way, you would not have spoken to me. Let me start by saying, I'm sorry. I'm sorry for the heartache you felt because of me. I'm sorry for the pain I caused. I apologize for letting you walk away when I did. But I'm not sorry for loving you then and now. Loving you enough then to let you know my heart was not in a place to accept you like you deserved. Loving you enough now to come back and ask you can we try again. Bae, I know I fucked up. I knew it the moment you walked out of my front door that day. But I had to do that so I could make sure when I came back to you, I was a better man. The man that I needed to be, the man who deserved you. A man whose heart is only filled by thoughts and love for you. When I was thinking about the decision to walk away from you, I talked to Greg. I told him how I felt about you. I told him that even though I had love for you, I knew at that time I wasn't any good for you. He said something to me that is still resolute in my mind. He said that 'no one wants a used car.' I thought he was full of shit when he said that but then he explained it to me. He said, 'That woman deserves a new car not a car that has a distressed engine and a bad transmission. If you love that woman like you say but you know that you are not in a place where you can be what she needs, don't be her used car. Let her go. When you have been renewed and restored with a new engine and transmission, then maybe you can go back to her. But don't damage her. She doesn't deserve that.' And he was right. It was the best thing for you and me. I knew if I had done it any other way, you would have stayed and that wasn't what was best. It wasn't fair to you."

"That's real cute and all but first off don't call me Bae. You lost that privilege a long time ago. Second, I didn't then and I don't need you now to tell me what was best for me. It was my decision to stay or go and you took that away from me. And third, you come here after three years thinking that my heart is still open for you?" I laugh a little and continue working on my dinner.

"You're right. I apologize for calling you Bae." He continues talking while looking trying to make eye contact. "You deserve a man who is going to love you completely. Not compare you to another or carry the active memories of another while being with you. I wasn't the man you needed back then but I knew what kind of woman you were. And I knew to be with you and be what you deserved I had to be better than what I had ever been."

"What's your point Shamar? You keep rambling on and on saying the same shit over and over again. Get to the point because your minute is about up."

"Peace, what I'm trying to say is this. After Jessica walked out on me, I thought that I would never recover or be able to love another woman in that way. I made the mistake in the beginning. I wasn't ready and I wasn't honest about it. I'm here to ask you for another chance. I'm here to show you that I know my heart only wants you. I've dated other women in the past few years. Some of them were good women but they were no match to you. I waited for my heart to grasp theirs but it never happened. It always came back to you. The time we shared, the laughs, the friendship, and the love. I loved you when you walked away from me the first time but I wasn't prepared for you. Not the amazing and powerful woman that you are. But now, today, I know that I am. I know that you are the one who has never left my heart. The one who has been in my dreams. The one who has filled that whole in my heart. And no one else can do that. I'm here to ask for another chance. Another chance to show you and prove to you what I'm saying is true."

As I begin to answer, the front door opens. "Baby, I'm home. Do we have company? Whose car is the driveway?"

Once again, he missed the signs. Shamar missed my wedding band set sitting on the side of the cutting board that I had taken off prior to prepping my dinner. He missed the pictures from my wedding on the walls in the foyer as he walked down the hall towards he kitchen. He missed the fact that he had to replace the flowers that were already in the vase with the flowers he brought for me. He missed it all. But now, he can't miss the fact that he's three years too late because the transitional woman he once knew is no longer holding that title. He looks at my face with wide eyes.

"Did you just expect for me to be waiting around for you for three years? Pining over you and hoping that you would come back. Crying every night and wondering who you were laying with?"

I look up and Shamar turns to see my husband walk into the kitchen. Yes, my husband. The man that walked into my life two years ago and renewed my belief in love and trust. The man that took my torn and broken heart and mended it without scars. The man who has accepted me with my faults and my attitude.

"Hi love." He says and walks over to kiss me softly. In his hand is a dozen white tulips. "I see we do have company." He reaches into the island cabinet and pulls out another vase for the tulips as he notices the roses in the table vase. He fills it with water, places the tulips inside, and leaves the vase on the countertop. "Baby, I didn't know you liked roses?"

"Love, you know tulips are my favorite. Yes, we do have company. Honey, this is Shamar. Shamar, this is my husband, Jeremiah." The men advance toward each other and shake hands.

"Shamar. Finally, we meet. I knew we would one day." Jeremiah smiles and returns by my side. "No need to cook dinner tonight love, I'll cook the stir-fry tomorrow. We're going out, I made reservations. I'm going to shower and change. I'll be ready in forty-five minutes."

"Should I change?" I ask him.

"You look beautiful Bae. No need to change anything." He says and kisses my forehead then walks back around the island. "It was nice to meet you Shamar." He extends his hand for a good-bye handshake, then leaves the kitchen to head down the long hallway to our bedroom and closes the door behind him.

"Damn." Shamar says and lowers his head and stands from the barstool. He looks at me one more time. "I guess I just made an ass of myself huh?"

"You did what you came here to do and you have the answers that you need."

"True. True. Honestly, I'm glad that you're happy and you found someone to love you."

"Actually, he found me just as it is intended. But thank you. I pray you find the same."

"So do I Peace. So do I." he says as we both head to the front door to say our final good-byes. He stops, turns around, and grabs my hands. He looks directly into my eyes and says, "I missed it."

There's nothing else for me to say. I look at him and shake my head. The silence between us is saying more than words can ever express. I lean in to kiss his cheek for the last time then step away and open the front door for him. Before he walks out, he raises his hand to touch my cheek. I back away. In his eyes, I see the tears forming and even though they don't fall, they are on the edge. He turns away and walks out the door. I close it behind him and walk away. From the kitchen, I can hear the gravel drive shift as he backs out.

"Good-bye Shamar."

Something to think about:

A very good friend said, "When your credit is good with God, He will not give you a used car. God will fashion you a new car because he wants you to have long-term happiness. Even if that used car is a good car and you're happy with that used car, once He sees that you are serious about that car, God will work on that car and repair it to make it new. And if that car is meant for you, He will send it back to you renewed. If it's not, the new car he fashions for you will have all the options He knows you want."

Through it all we live and we learn from our experiences with others and time spent with ourselves. This piece of work is fictional in nature with personal events intertwined from my own experiences. Am I the true "Transitional Woman," it's a possibility. Don't feel sorry for the possibility because some of you have related to the events in this short story too. Remember there's a little bit of the that woman in all of us.

Thank You All

Thank you all for taking the time to read this story and taking this ride with me from time to time. I send a prayer of love and blessings to you all. If there was something that you got from this book, please let me know.

IG: Tanik176   Facebook: Tanisha N Bowman

Amazon: Please leave a comment under the title.

Colossians 3:12-14

Therefore, as God's chosen people, holy and dearly loved, clothe yourselves with compassion, kindness, humility, gentleness and patience. Bear with each other and forgive one another if any of you has a grievance against someone. Forgive as the Lord forgave you. And over all these virtues put on love, which binds them all together in perfect unity.